Always Be Charming from A to Z

Written and Illustrated by
Rhonda Stovall West

ABC Company

Always Be Charming from A to Z
© 2010 by Rhonda Stovall West

Printed in the U.S.A.

ISBN: 978-0-9645540-0-9

Edited by Chloé R. Broom

First Edition

Thank you

Special thank you

To my husband Ronald D. West and children Jermaine, Rick, Chloé and Randall for continuing to believe in me. To my granddaughters, Deveney and Rikki, thank you for your enthusiasm and eagerness to help. Many thanks to my parents Robert (Roy) and Billie J. Stovall without them my whole life would not have been possible. To my sister Tina Ransom and brother-in-law Lamont Ransom for their inspiration, thank you. To my sister Candace Stovall-Henry and brother Michael Stovall thank you for all your support.

And

To Myrna Johnson, Thomas Knight, and Gwendolyn Lane, Mary Jackson, Shirley Freeman, Rossalyn Gordon, whose time and assistance were invaluable in making this book possible, I will always be grateful. To Marcie Rehmer, who for ten years helped in the development of my speaking career at Nationwide Children's Hospital. To Roseanne Schoenbachler, whose warmth and charming sense of humor often encouraged me to continue writing when I felt like giving up. To Carol Triggs, thank you for believing in my ability to communicate this message. To Judy Pitts, Kathy Lancaster, Michelle Charity, Jamie McCardle-Blair, Claudia Barrett, Carole Witcher, Marilyn Francine Barnett Morgan, Germain Gilton, Donald Nelson Jr., and Bea Foster your helpful suggestions were an inspiration. To Denney Kiner, and Jessica Vandermark, JáLil Person, Kimberly J.L. Person, Jr., Charette Johnson, and Kurt Shade, Sr. whose expert computer skills helped me to improve mine. To Dr. Quander L. Wilson, Sr. thank you for the wisdom you spoke into my life, for believing in me and praying for me.

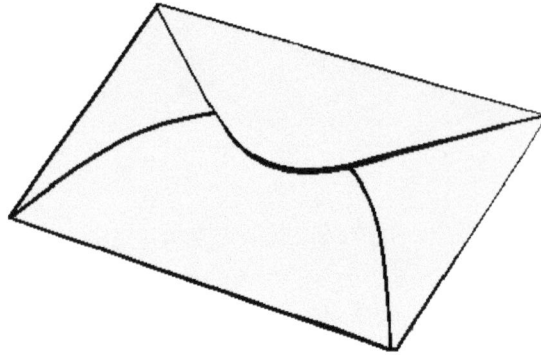

Dedicated to my charming MOM, Billie Jean Stovall, who taught me well.

Inspired by my daughter Chloé, who like me strives daily to always be charming.

— R.S.W.

A NOTE FROM THE AUTHOR

Dear Reader,

This book is about a charming young girl named Chloé who strives daily to be her personal best. She is very busy, but always finds time to encourage others. Chloé believes inside every little girl is a beauty queen. All they need is to believe it too. Taking on the persona and owning it, Chloe' morphs into Miss ABC. Share her world and helpful tips to bring out the best in you. Like Chloé no matter what, live your dream and hold on to your crown beauty queen!

Love
Rhonda

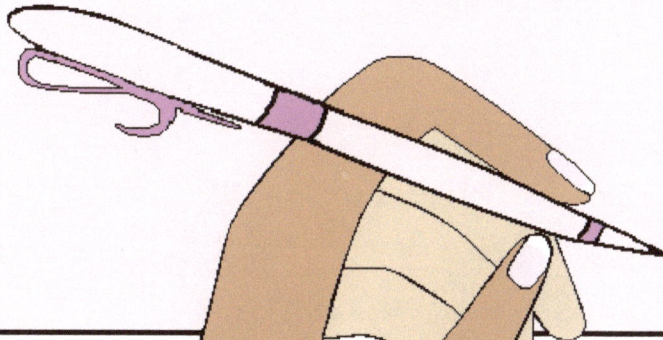

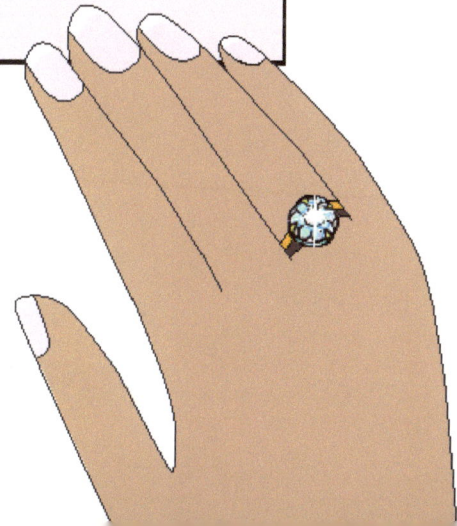

INTERN

Attitude — expressing your thoughts and feelings to others.

Getting along with others is key, give it a try and you will surely see. Have a pleasant personality and a positive way of thinking. Put a smile in your voice when you are speaking. You will sound more cheerful, friendly, and polite. People enjoy being around those who are such a delight.

Behavior — your personal conduct.

Whether you are at home, school, or in the community model the behavior you expect by treating others with the same respect. There is nothing attractive about causing distractions. Be cool, calm and in control of your thoughts, words, and reactions.

ABC=
Always Be Charming

Cleanliness — washing away dirt.

It is good to be clean. Make it a part of your daily routine. A clean body and mind will make you feel energized and refreshed. Comb your hair, brush your teeth, and put on clothes that are clean and pressed.

Determination — sticking to your plan.

Never give up on what you set out to do. Accomplishing your goals is completely up to you. No matter how many times you fail, try harder to go farther. Do not be discouraged. Stay on track and have courage! You will get better in time. Focus on the finish line.

FINISH

ABC

Chloé

80

Etiquette — the customary rules for socially acceptable behavior.

Good manners are essential for your social success. It is a never-ending process. Whether you are at home or at the café to your family and everyone, be courteous every day.

Fitness — the act of working to make your body healthy and strong.

Exercise regularly to stay in good physical condition, include a friend; they would be a great addition. Play a sport, walk, or run. Being fit can be lots of fun!

Gracefulness — using your body as an instrument of beauty.

Body language and facial expression make a lasting impression. Your every movement has relevance. Like the beauty and softness of a ballet dancer always move with such grace and elegance.

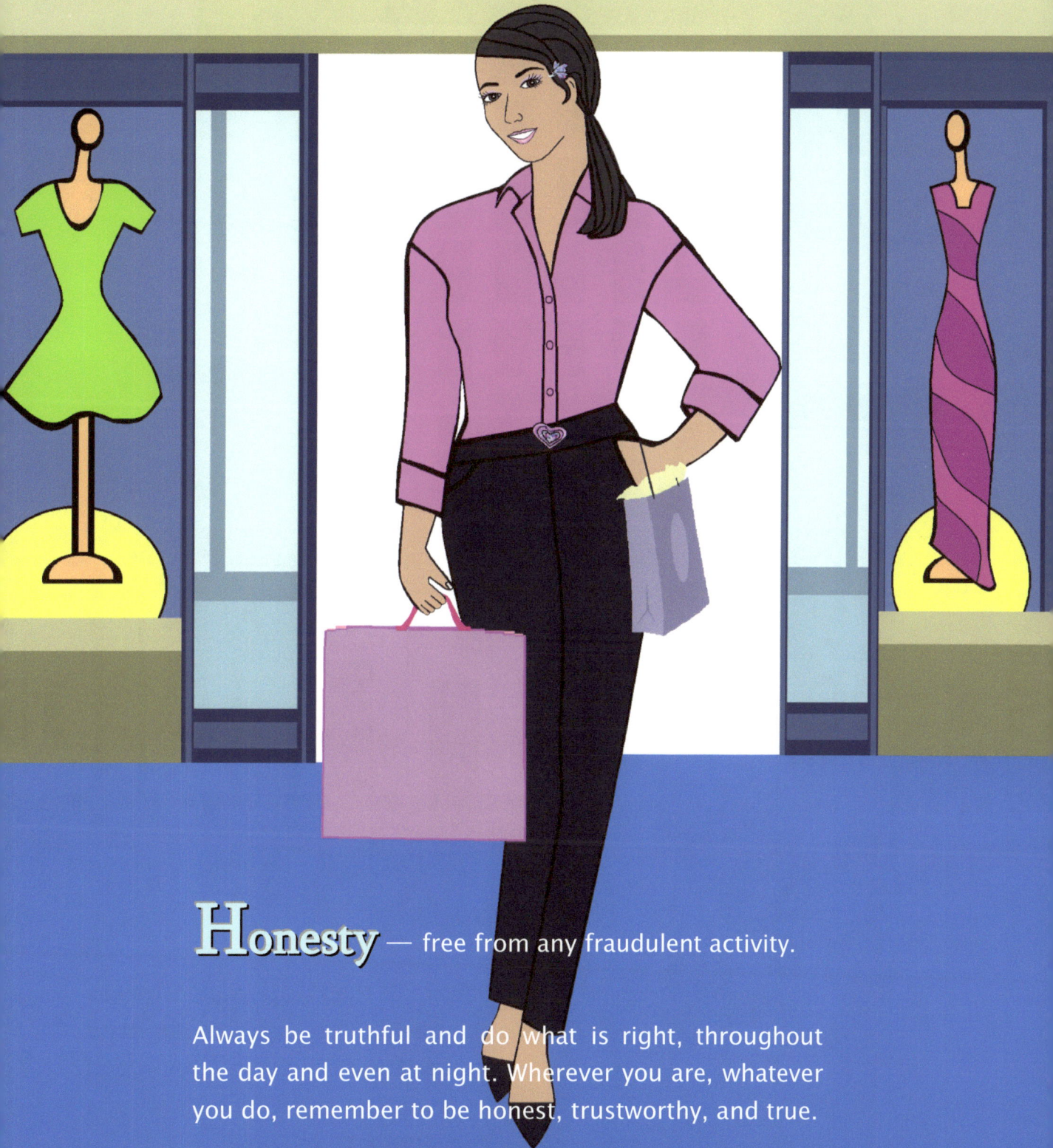

Honesty — free from any fraudulent activity.

Always be truthful and do what is right, throughout the day and even at night. Wherever you are, whatever you do, remember to be honest, trustworthy, and true.

Integrity — exhibiting moral character.

Be aware of the image you portray as a member of society. Aim to stand out in a positive way. A good reputation is nice to know, it follows you everywhere you go.

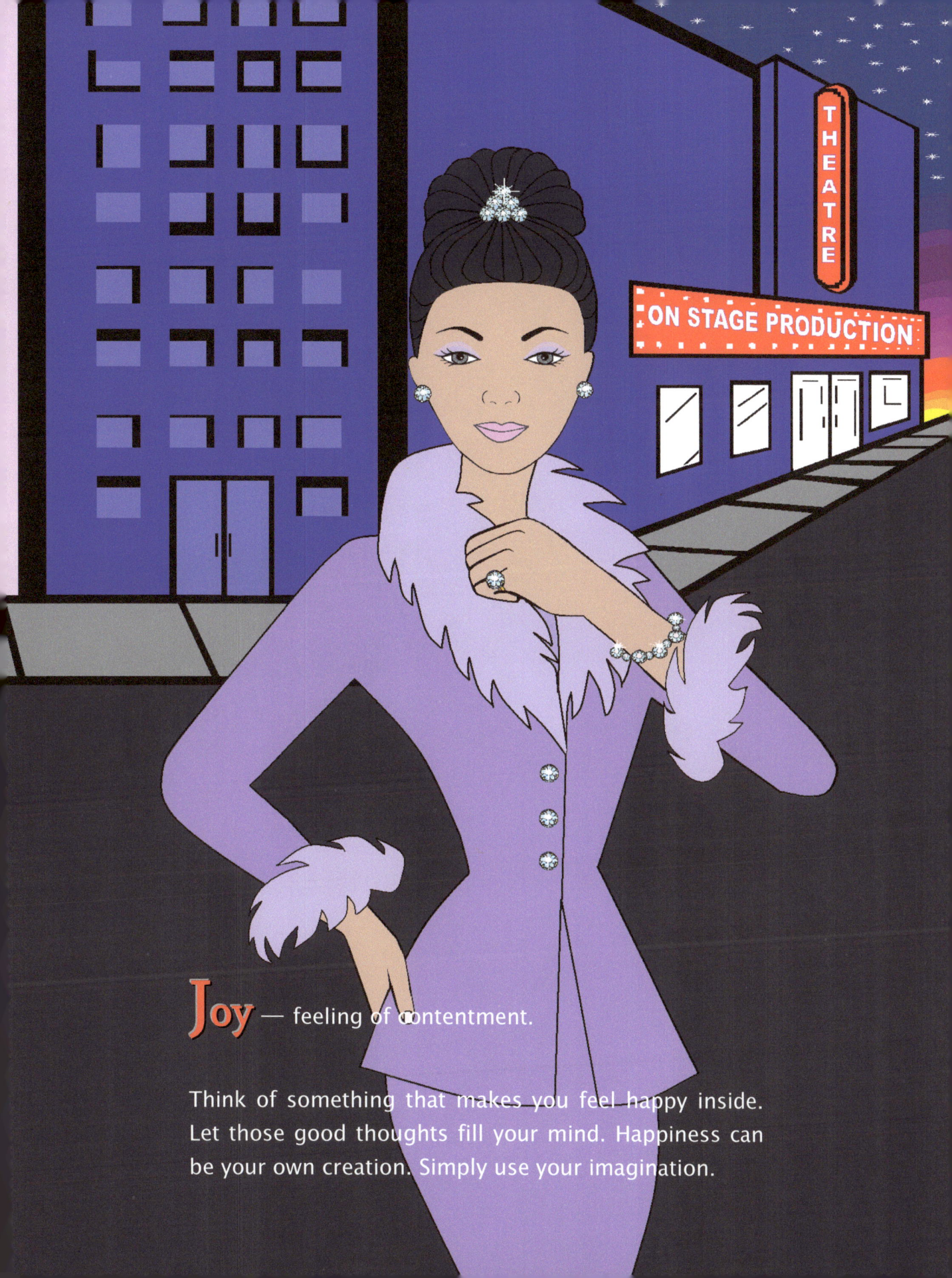

Joy — feeling of contentment.

Think of something that makes you feel happy inside.
Let those good thoughts fill your mind. Happiness can
be your own creation. Simply use your imagination.

Knowledge — things you learn throughout your life.

Never stop learning; if you refuse to learn, you refuse to succeed. Do not be afraid to ask for the kind of information you want and need. Reading helps to increase your vocabulary. There is a variety of fun and interesting books at the library.

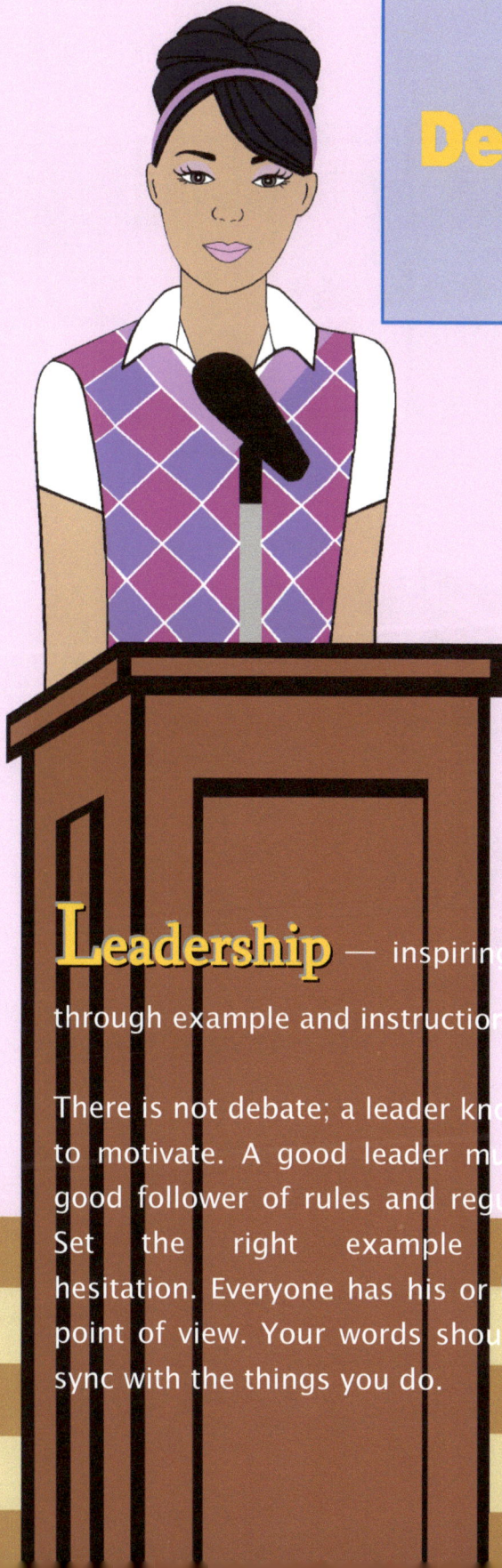

Leadership — inspiring others through example and instruction.

There is not debate; a leader knows how to motivate. A good leader must be a good follower of rules and regulations. Set the right example without hesitation. Everyone has his or her own point of view. Your words should be in sync with the things you do.

Motivation — having the initiative to follow through on a task.

Be your own biggest cheerleader for your personal satisfaction. Motivate yourself to take action. Eliminate negativity. Explore a new and exciting activity. Keep a positive frame of mind. You will make new friends and have fun all at the same time.

Nutrition — food and nourishment for your body.

Eating healthy is wise. A well balanced diet can add shine to your hair, strengthen your teeth; put a glow in your skin and a sparkle in your eyes.

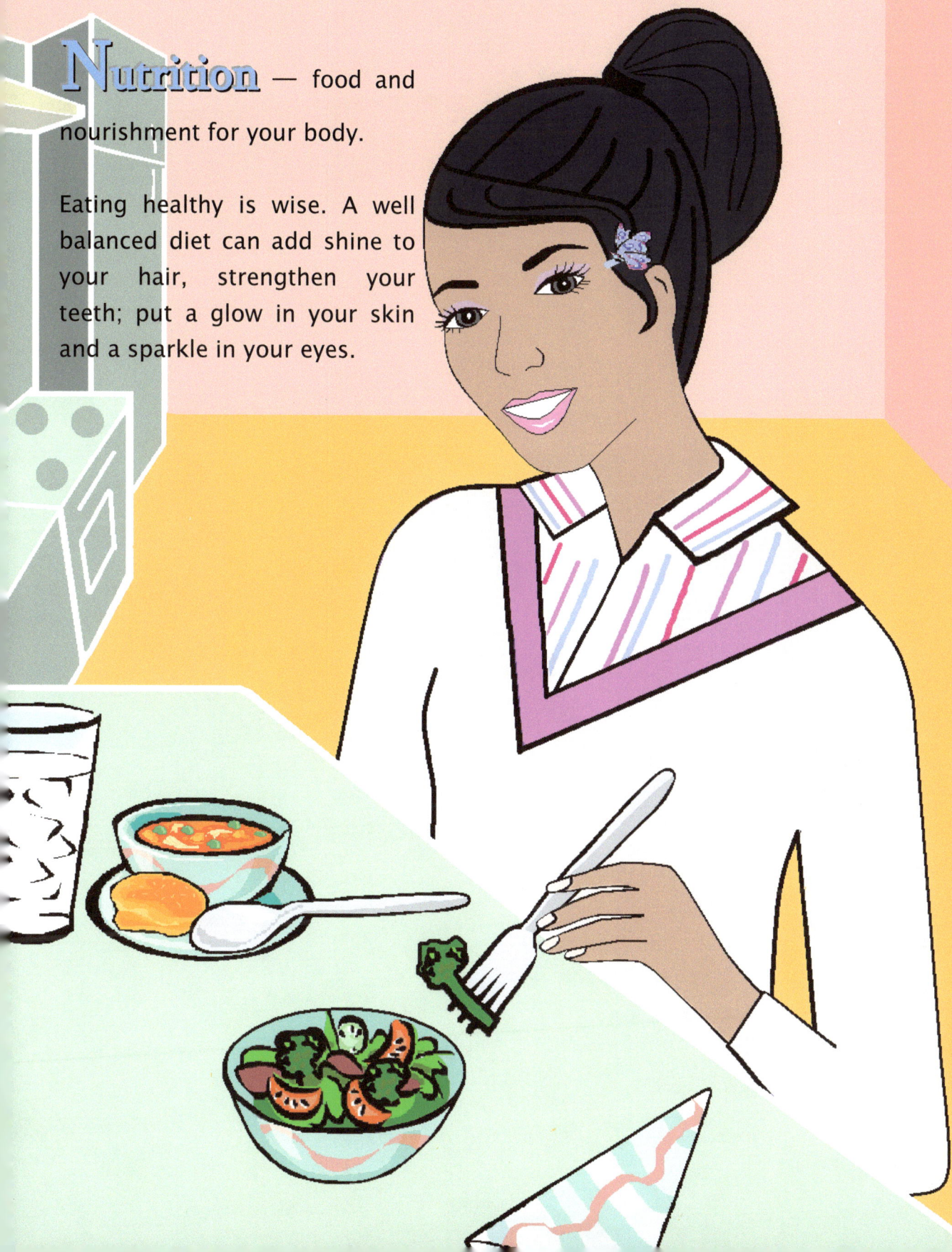

Est. 1980
ABC School

Organize — to plan your time well and put things in order to be prepared.

Each day is filled with something new, many places to go and things to do. You will not have to look very far when you know where all your things are. Time is precious; you do not want to be late. It is impolite to make others wait.

Poise — good posture.

Grace and poise go hand in hand. It is how you walk and talk and sit and stand. It is looking at people directly in the eye; not aimlessly staring down. It is holding your neck and back straight as if you were wearing a crown.

SCIENCE

ARTS

SERVICE

Chloé

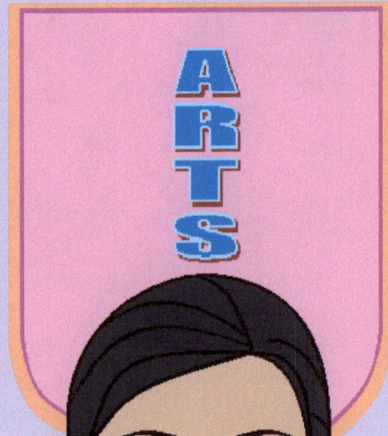

Quality — putting forth the standard of excellence.

Whatever you do, you should always do your very best! It takes hard work to reap the rewards and benefits of success. You have what it takes. Learn from your mistakes. Practice over and over day and night. Before you know it you will get it right.

Responsibility — something you are to take charge of.

Always take care of your duties; do not wait to be told to do a chore. Doing them on your own means so much more. Finish your tasks before having fun and you will be pleased with another job well done. Working with a happy heart makes it easier and that is smart.

Things to do...

AMBITION AVENUE | RIGHT ROAD

DESTINY DRIVE | SUCCESS STREET

PURPOSE PLACE | WINNING WAY

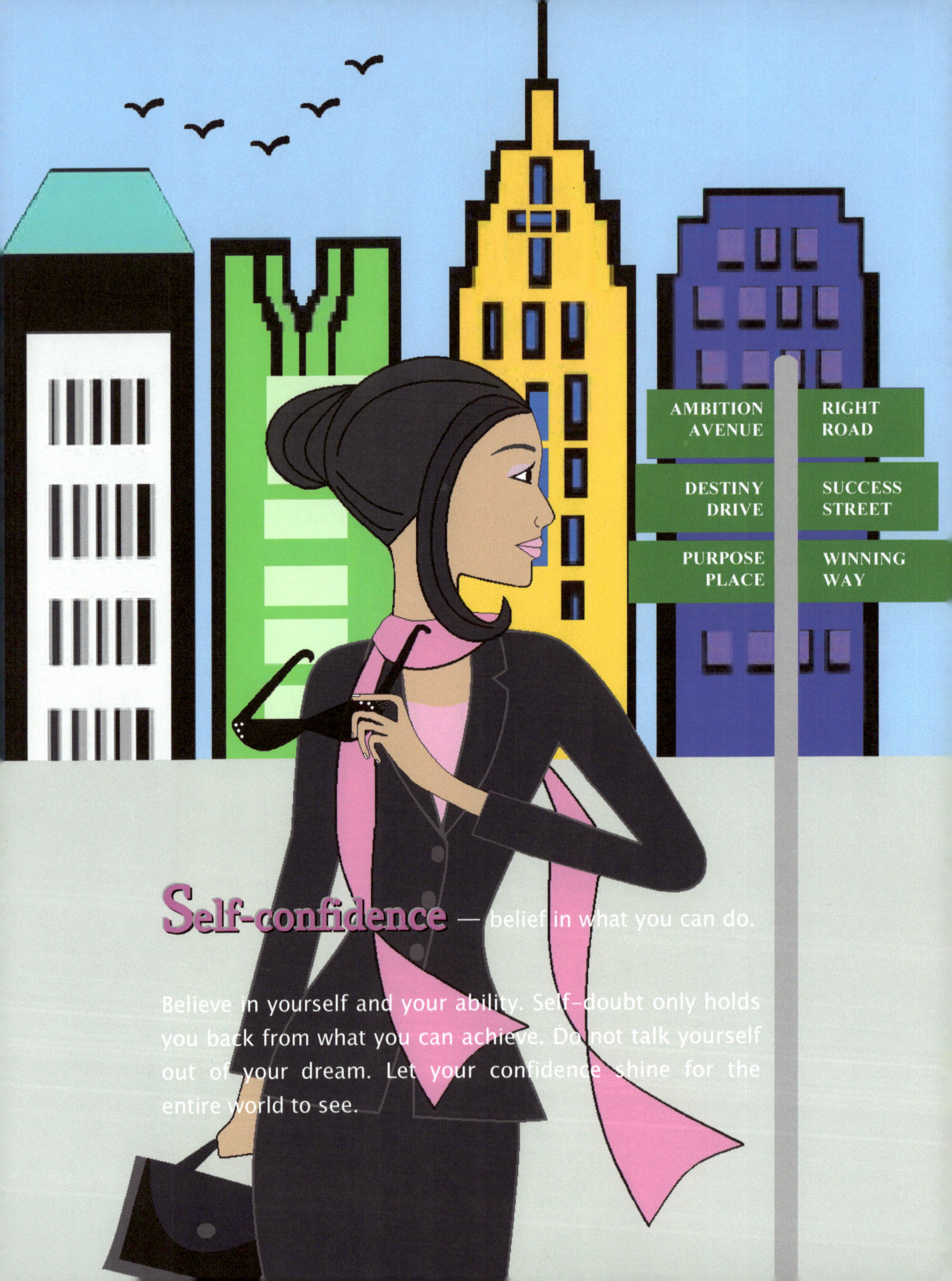

Self-confidence — belief in what you can do.

Believe in yourself and your ability. Self-doubt only holds you back from what you can achieve. Do not talk yourself out of your dream. Let your confidence shine for the entire world to see.

Thoughtfulness — being nice and generous towards others.

"Have a good day", "Thank you" and "Please" are words that spread kindness and put others at ease. Like planting a garden show you care by treating people just and fair. Sometimes all it takes is a smiling, warm face to make the world a better place.

Unlimited — that which is never ending.

Never let anyone shoot down your dream because they think it is too extreme. The sky is the limit aim higher and higher. Rest assured you can obtain your desire.

JUDGE CHLOÉ

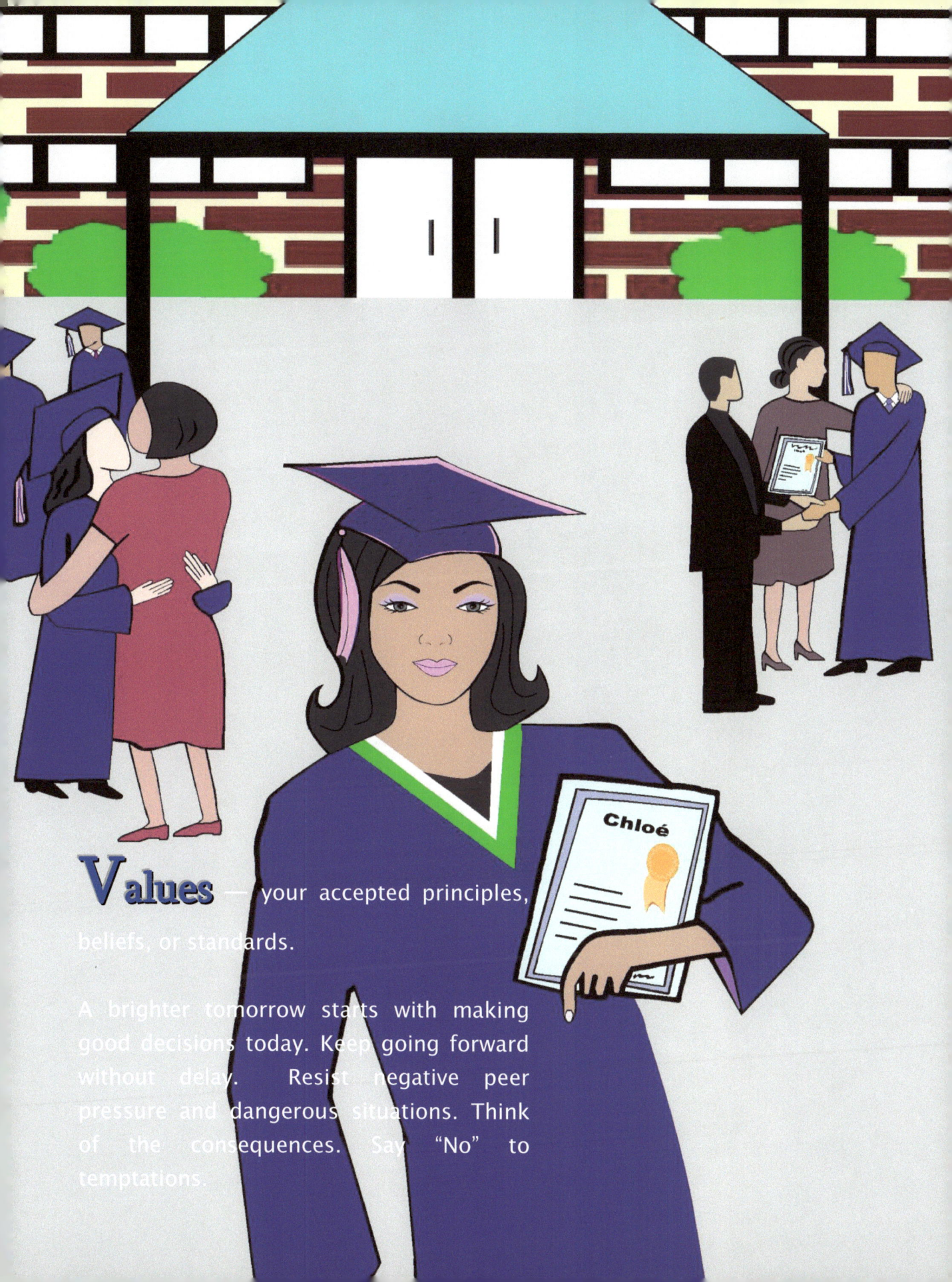

Values — your accepted principles, beliefs, or standards.

A brighter tomorrow starts with making good decisions today. Keep going forward without delay. Resist negative peer pressure and dangerous situations. Think of the consequences. Say "No" to temptations.

Winning — to be victorious.

A real winner knows how to win and lose with grace. First, second, or third take your place. Show everyone that you have style with good sportsmanship and a winning smile.

X-ray — making a mental photograph of your inner self.

Without a doubt true beauty comes from the inside out. Focus your thoughts on what is in your mind and heart. That is the perfect place to start. What lies beneath shows in your eyes, your smile and your personality. It reflects all the things you truly aspire to be.

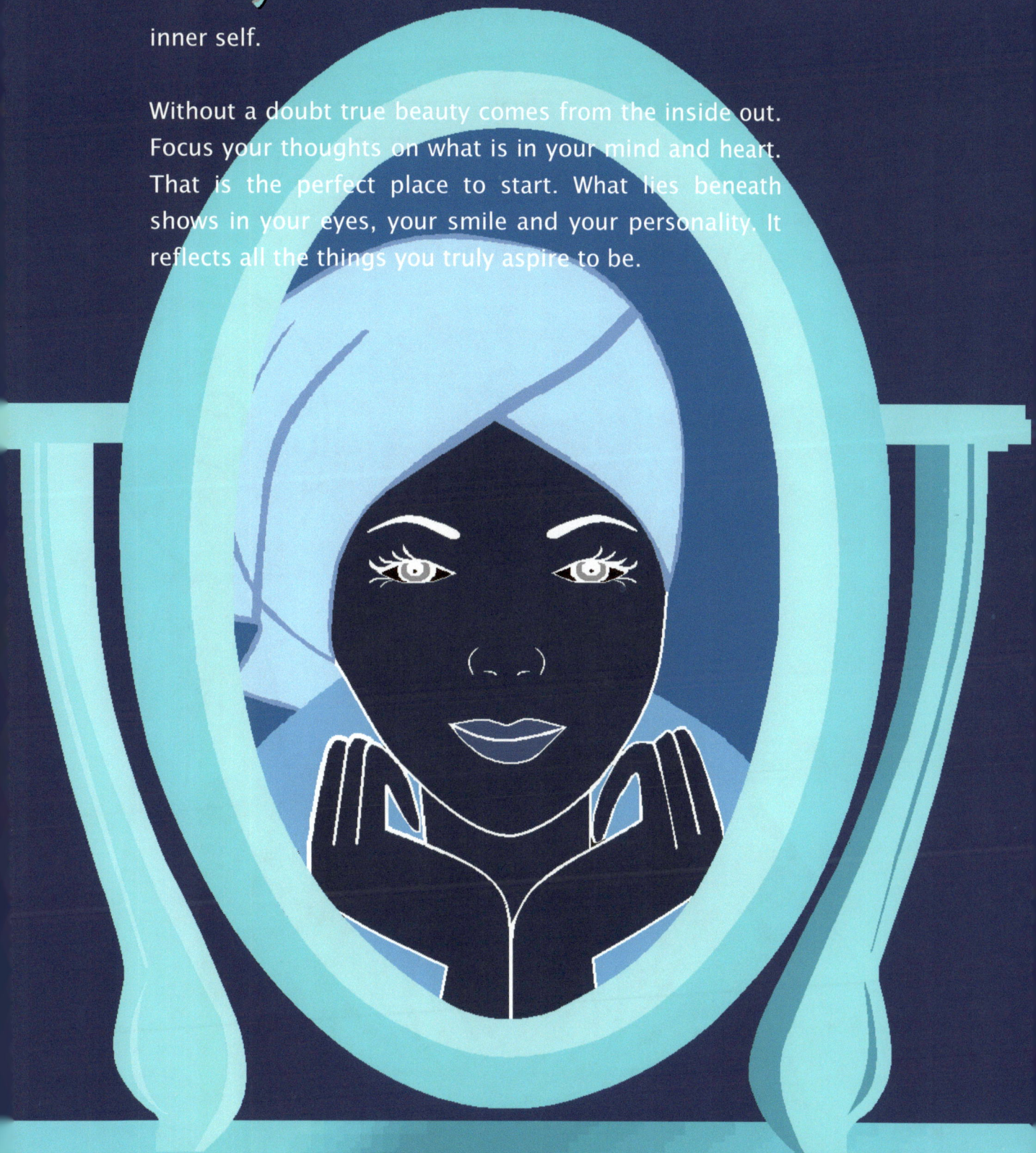

You — the one these words are written to.

We all tend to follow a certain trend whether it is fashion, food, or attitude. It is okay to borrow ideas from someone else. Most importantly you must be yourself. Do not be ashamed of who you are. Be your best and you will go far.

Zeal — passion for crowning achievements.

Start now and do everything in your power to hold on to your dream. Hopefully these hints will help you to achieve your goals and gain more self-esteem. You are a winner in my book. Learn something new every time you take a look.

*Best wishes and as always…
be charming!*

www.ingramcontent.com/pod-product-compliance
Lightning Source LLC
Chambersburg PA
CBHW041238040426

42445CB00004B/74